MACMILLAN READERS
ELEMENTARY

D1536911

SUSAN HILL

The Woman in Black

Retold by Margaret Tarner

MACMILLAN

ELEMENTARY LEVEL

Founding Editor: John Milne

The Macmillan Readers provide a choice of enjoyable reading materials for learners of English. The series is published at six levels – Starter, Beginner, Elementary, Pre-intermediate, Intermediate and Upper.

Level control

Information, structure and vocabulary are controlled to suit the students' ability at each level.

The number of words at each level:

Starter	about 300 basic words
Beginner	about 600 basic words
Elementary	about 1100 basic words
Pre-intermediate	about 1400 basic words
Intermediate	about 1600 basic words
Upper	about 2200 basic words

Vocabulary

Some difficult words and phrases in this book are important for understanding the story. Some of these words are explained in the story and some are shown in the pictures. From Pre-intermediate level upwards, words are marked with a number like this: ...[3]. These words are explained in the Glossary at the end of the book.

Contents

A Note About This Story

This story is set in England, many years ago. At this time, London often had bad fogs in the winter. This fog was a very thick, dirty mist. The fog mixed with the smoke from fires and factories. It was difficult to see or breathe in these fogs.

Arthur Kipps is the hero in this story. In Chapter 2, Arthur is twenty-three years old. He is soon to be married. His *fiancée*, the woman he is going to marry, is called Stella.

Arthur works as a *solicitor* in London. He helps people with their legal business. For example, he writes the documents when land or buildings are bought or sold. He also prepares *wills*. These papers say who people want to give their money or property to when they die. When someone dies, the solicitor sometimes goes to their *funeral*. Later, the solicitor arranges for their money or property to be given to the dead person's family.

1

Christmas Eve

My name is Arthur Kipps. When I was a young man, I worked in London. I was a solicitor. I worked for the same company all my life.

Fourteen years ago, I bought this house called Monk's Piece. I live here with my dear wife, Esmé.

Esmé's first husband had died. She was a widow when I married her. I became the father of her four young children. Our years at Monk's Piece have been happy ones.

It was Christmas Eve. All the family were at Monk's Piece for the holiday. We were all sitting by the big fire at the end of the day.

I was in my armchair, listening to the laughter and the talking.

'Wake up, Father!' someone called. 'We're going to tell ghost stories!'

The lights were turned off. Suddenly the room was dark and shadowy. I smiled as I listened to the young people's stories. The stories were full of horror, but they did not frighten me. They were not true.

Then I remembered. I remembered terrible things. These memories were terrible – because they were true!

'Tell us a ghost story, Father!' someone cried. 'You must know one story!'

I stood up, cold and shaking.

'No, no!' I shouted. 'I have no story to tell!'

'No, no!' I shouted. 'I have no story to tell!'

I hurried from the room, away from them all. I went out into the garden. I stood there in the cold and in the darkness. My heart was beating fast. I was shaking with fear. Will I never forget? Will I never find peace?

How can I find peace? There is only one way. I must write down my terrible story. All the horror. Everything. Then I will find peace.

I turned and walked back into the house.

2

London Fog

My story begins in November, many years ago. I was a young man of twenty-three. I worked for a solicitor called Mr Bentley. Sometimes the work was uninteresting, but I worked hard. I wanted to do well.

That November morning, the weather was cold. A thick, yellow fog covered London. The fog filled people's ears and eyes. It got into houses, shops and offices.

Mr Bentley called me into his office.

'Sit down, Arthur, sit down,' Mr Bentley said. He pointed to a paper on his desk.

'This is the will of Mrs Drablow. Mrs Alice Drablow of Eel Marsh House in Yorkshire. A strange old lady and a strange house. Have you ever been to Yorkshire, Arthur?'

'No, sir.'

'Well, my boy, go home and pack your bag. Mrs Drablow is dead. She has no relatives in England. And we are her solicitors. I want you to go to the funeral.'

Mr Bentley saw that I was surprised. 'I can't go myself,' Mr Bentley said quickly. 'I'm too busy.'

'After the funeral,' he went on, 'I want you to go to Eel Marsh House. I want you to look at the old lady's papers. Bring back anything important.'

Mr Bentley stood up.

'The funeral's at eleven o'clock tomorrow morning,' he said. 'Take the afternoon train from King's Cross Station. Here is the key to Eel Marsh House. Mrs Drablow's will and other important papers are in this envelope.'

And he held out a large, brown envelope. Written on the front of the envelope was: *Mrs Alice Drablow, Eel Marsh House, Nine Lives Causeway, Crythin Gifford, Yorkshire.*

'What a strange address!' I said.

'Yes, it's a strange address and it's a strange place,' Mr Bentley said. 'Now off you go, my boy.'

There wasn't much time to get ready for the journey. I quickly packed my bag. Then I wrote a note to Stella, my fiancée. Then I set off for King's Cross Station.

The fog was thicker now. The smell of fog was everywhere. At last I reached the big, noisy station. I was beginning to feel excited. I was going on a journey. I had an important job to do.

I was soon sitting in the train. And then it was moving. Slowly at first and then faster. The fog of London was left behind. Darkness fell. I was on my way north – to Eel Marsh House.

I changed trains at Crewe. Then I changed trains again at a small town called Homerby, in Yorkshire. The air was cold. The wind blew rain on my face.

The little train I got into at Homerby was old and dirty. I put the brown envelope on the seat beside me. I opened my newspaper and began to read.

A few minutes later, a big man with a red face got into the carriage. He sat down as the train began to move out of Homerby.

'It's cold in here,' I said. 'But I've left the fog of London behind me.'

'We don't have fogs here. We have mists. The mists come in from the sea,' the big man said.

We sat for a few moments in silence. Then I saw the big man look at the envelope on the seat beside me.

'Drablow,' he said. 'Are you a relative?'

'No, I'm a solicitor,' I said. 'I'm going to the funeral.'

'You'll be the only one there, Mr . . .?'

'My name's Kipps, Arthur Kipps,' I told him.

'I'm Samuel Daily,' the big man said.

'Didn't Mrs Drablow have any friends?' I asked.

'No, she didn't have any friends,' Mr Daily said. 'People become strange when they live in strange places.'

I smiled.

'Are you trying to frighten me, Mr Daily?' I asked.

He stared at me.

'No, I'm not trying to frighten you,' he said. 'But there are other people in Crythin Gifford who will try to frighten you.'

I suddenly felt very cold.

'Where are you staying tonight?' Mr Daily asked me.

'I'm going to stay at the Gifford Arms.'

'The Gifford Arms is a comfortable inn,' said Mr Daily. 'I go past it on my way home. You can come with me in my car.'

Mr Daily's car was waiting at the station. A few minutes later, it stopped outside the inn. Mr Daily gave me his card with his address on it.

'That's where I live,' he said. 'If you need any help, come and see me.'

The Gifford Arms was warm and comfortable. After a good supper, I went to bed.

I slept well. Thank God I did. I never slept so well again.

3

The Funeral of Mrs Drablow

The next morning was bright and sunny. I ate a good breakfast. Then I walked round the little town of Crythin Gifford. It was market-day. The little town was busy. Farmers were buying and selling animals in the market-square.

The streets of Crythin Gifford were completely flat. The countryside all round the town was flat too. There were no hills at all. To the east of the town were the marshes – and on the marshes was Eel Marsh House.

I walked back to the inn and got ready for the funeral. I put on a dark suit and went downstairs again.

Mr Jerome was waiting for me downstairs. Mr Jerome was Mrs Drablow's agent – he looked after her house and land. Mr Jerome was a small man dressed in black. He smiled politely and we left the inn.

As we walked through the square, people stared at us. They stopped talking. No one smiled.

The church stood in an old graveyard. There were old gravestones on either side of a long path.

It was very cold inside the church. Mr Jerome and I were the only people at the funeral. Poor Mrs Drablow, I thought. Didn't she have any friends at all? Then I heard a sound behind me.

I turned. A young woman was standing at the back of the church. She was dressed in old-fashioned black clothes – clothes of sixty years ago. A large, old-fashioned bonnet covered her face. She raised her head and looked at me. The young woman's face was white and very thin. How ill she looked!

When we left the church I looked for the woman. But I did not see her. Then in the graveyard, I saw her again. In the sunshine her face was whiter and thinner.

I closed my eyes to pray. When I opened them, the woman had gone. Beyond the graveyard I saw the estuary. And beyond the estuary was the open sea.

The funeral was over. I followed Mr Jerome from the churchyard.

'Who was that young woman?' I asked him.

Mr Jerome stopped and looked at me.

'Young woman?' he said.

'Yes, a young woman. She was dressed in black and she looked very ill.'

Mr Jerome's face went white.

'I did not see a young woman,' he said.

I looked behind me. The young woman was standing beside Mrs Drablow's grave.

'Look, there she is!' I said.

The young woman was standing beside Mrs Drablow's grave.

Mr Jerome made a strange sound. He did not turn round to look at the woman. He held my arm tightly. He began to shake.

'Mr Jerome!' I cried. 'Are you ill? Let go of my arm and I'll bring a car for you.'

'No, no,' he cried. 'No, sir. Stay with me!'

After a few moments, Mr Jerome spoke again.

'I'm very sorry, sir,' he said quietly. 'I felt ill for a moment. I can go on now.'

We walked slowly back to the Gifford Arms.

'Are you taking me to Eel Marsh House, Mr Jerome?' I said politely.

The little man shook his head.

'No, not me,' he said. 'Keckwick will take you. You have to go across a causeway to get to Eel Marsh House. When the tide is in, the sea covers the causeway. You can't get across. You can only cross the causeway when the tide is out. That will be after one o'clock.'

'There may be a lot of papers to look at,' I said. 'I may stay in Eel Marsh House tonight.'

'You will find the inn more comfortable,' Mr Jerome said quietly.

'Perhaps you are right,' I said.

The lunch at the Gifford Arms was a good one and I ate well.

At half past one, I was waiting outside the inn. The key to Eel Marsh House was in my pocket. I listened for the sound of Keckwick's car.

4

Eel Marsh House

After a few minutes, a pony and trap came into the square. It stopped beside me.

'Mr Kipps?' the driver said.

'Are you Keckwick?' I asked. I was surprised that Keckwick did not come in a car.

The man nodded his head.

I got into the trap. The pony started off at once.

We drove quickly through the quiet little town. We passed the churchyard and were soon in open country.

The country around the town was completely flat. There was a beautiful, grey sky above us.

After a time, we reached the marshes. The marshes were strange and beautiful. No trees grew in the marshes. There was water everywhere. There were no people and no houses. There was silence. The only sound was the noise made by the hooves of the pony and the wheels of the trap.

We drove along the path until we came to the causeway. The long causeway went across the estuary. The sandy causeway was not much higher than the water on each side.

This is Nine Lives Causeway, I thought. At high tide the water will completely cover it.

The bright winter sun shone in my eyes. I shut them for a moment.

When I opened my eyes, we were near the end of the causeway. In front of us was a tall, grey house. It stood alone looking over the marshes and the water of the estuary.

In front of us was a tall, grey house.

The lonely house was on a little island. This was Eel Marsh House!

The trap stopped in front of the house. For a few moments I did not move. What a strange, lonely place! But the place was so beautiful that I did not feel afraid.

I got out of the trap.

'When will the water cover the causeway again?'

'In two hours,' Keckwick answered.

I did not want to leave so soon. I wanted more time in this beautiful place.

'Two hours won't be enough time for me to do my work here,' I said. 'I'll come back here again tomorrow. I'll bring food and drink with me and stay for a day or two. But now that I'm here, I'll have a look round the house. What are you going to do? Will you wait here or come back for me later?'

Keckwick did not answer. He turned the pony and trap round and drove off. I watched the trap going back across the causeway. I was alone.

I stood there without moving. The key to the house was in my hand. A sea-bird flew by. It gave a cry. Then there was silence again.

What a place to live! I thought. Perhaps, one day, Stella and I will stay here. I wanted to be with her in this beautiful place.

There was a field behind the house. It went from the house to the water. The setting sun made the water red. The wind from the sea was getting colder.

At the end of the field, I saw a little church. It looked very old. It had no roof and its walls were broken. Some old gravestones stood round the old building.

It was beginning to grow dark. It was time to go inside the house.

And then I saw the young woman again. She was standing beside one of the gravestones. It was the woman in black. She was wearing the same old-fashioned clothes. She looked pale and ill. Her eyes were dark in her pale face.

Those eyes! How can I describe them? Her eyes were evil. They stared at me with a terrible hate. There was something the woman wanted from me – something she had lost. What was it?

I began to shake with fear. I felt very cold. My heart beat faster and faster. I wanted to run. But I was not able to move. What was wrong with me?

The woman stepped behind the gravestone. She had gone. My fear left me.

I ran down into the graveyard. I looked for the young woman everywhere. But she had disappeared.

There were the marshes. And there was the shining causeway. I was able to see for miles. But there were no houses. There was no place to hide. I did not understand it.

Suddenly my fear returned. I ran back to the house. I did not look back. I was too frightened to look back!

I reached the house and tried to open the door. My hand was shaking. At last the key was in the lock.

I opened the door and stepped inside. The door shut with a bang. The sound went through the empty house.

What had happened to me? Who was the woman in black? I did not believe in ghosts. But I had seen one. A ghost that was evil and terrible.

But I was inside the house now. I was safe. I smiled. I did not believe in ghosts. I had work to do. And I wanted to do it well. I must forget the woman in black.

I looked around. I was standing in a dark hallway. In front of me was a wide staircase. On one side was a passage.

Perhaps it led to the kitchen. There were several doors, all of them closed.

It was getting darker. I switched on a light in the hall. I went to the nearest door and opened it. I then opened one door after another. One door was locked.

There was old furniture in every room. It was all large and heavy. There were old pictures on all the walls. Every room had desks and cupboards. And my job was to look through all of them!

There was a damp smell in the house. Some of the rooms had not been used for many years. The whole house was dark and shadowy. Mrs Drablow had lived here alone, I thought. I was not surprised that people said she was strange!

I pulled up the blinds at every window. From each window I was able to see the marshes and the estuary. It was a beautiful place. But silent and lonely!

I used the keys to open some desks and cupboards. All of them were full of papers. I was sure that some of these papers were important. I had to look at all of them. This job will take a long time, I thought.

It was too late to start work that afternoon. I looked at my watch. Keckwick was not coming back for another hour.

I decided to walk back along the causeway. I was able to see the path from the window. It went straight ahead. It was not possible for me to lose my way. I was sure to meet Keckwick on the way.

I went back into every room. I pulled down the blinds. I turned off all the lights. I locked the front door behind me.

Then I started to walk along the causeway.

5

The Cry of a Child

Outside the house, everything was quiet. I looked back once, but I did not see the woman in black.

The causeway was dry. But the tide was coming in. The water on either side of the causeway was higher now. As I walked on, I felt very alone. The path over the causeway seemed longer too. I walked faster.

The sky and the water were beautiful in the grey light. Then I saw the sea-mist. The sea-mist was moving quickly over the marshes. In a few moments, the sea-mist covered everything.

It was a damp, white mist. It was very different from the yellow fog of London. The mist moved about in front of my eyes. Soon my hair and clothes were wet.

Now I saw only a short way in front of me. I looked back. I was not able to see Eel Marsh House. It had completely disappeared in the mist.

I walked on, very slowly. Then I stopped. If I went on, I might walk off the causeway into the deep mud. I decided to go back.

But going back was difficult too. The mist was moving all round me. Where was the house? Was I going the right way? I felt very afraid.

And then I heard the pony and trap. Thank God! Keckwick was coming back for me. I stopped and waited. But now the sounds of the pony and trap were going away from me. Now the sound was coming from somewhere on the marshes. What was wrong? Had Keckwick gone off the path?

I stood very still. For a moment, there was complete silence.

Suddenly a pony shrieked with fear. Then I heard a sound I shall never forget. The terrible cry of a child. A child in fear of death.

And now the trap was sinking. There was a strange sucking sound. The trap was going down under the mud. And still the child cried out.

There was nothing I could do! I shouted. But no one answered. How could I find the trap in that terrible mist? It was impossible.

I had to get back to the house. If I turned on all the lights, someone might see them. Someone might help.

It was dark now. The mist was thicker too. I heard the sea-water moving nearer.

At last I was standing on hard ground in front of the house. I found the front door and opened it. Behind me the marshes were silent.

I sat down on the nearest chair. I began to shake. Oh, the horror of that terrible cry! That poor child dying in the marshes. I began crying and was not able to stop.

After a time, I made myself stand up. I walked into every room and turned on the lights.

I found some brandy in a cupboard. I drank some and my fear turned to anger. Why had Mr Bentley sent me here? Why had I left London?

I walked in and out of the rooms. I wanted only one thing. I wanted to get away from this terrible place.

I walked slowly along a passage on the second floor. The door at the end was locked. I kicked the door angrily. But it did not open. I turned away and walked back.

As I went, I looked through every window. The white

Suddenly a pony shrieked with fear.

sea-mist was all around the house. I could see nothing.

I drank some more brandy. The brandy helped me to forget. To forget that terrible sound of the child crying. At last I fell asleep.

A bell was ringing. It rang again and again. I opened my eyes slowly. I looked through the window. The moon shone white in the black sky.

How long had I been asleep? I did not know. The bell rang again.

Then I remembered with horror the sound I had heard. I remembered the screams of the child. I remembered the shrieks of the pony. I remembered the noise of the trap as it sank down in the mud.

Had I heard those noises? Had I dreamt them? I did not know.

The bell rang again. Someone was at the door. Who was there? All the lights in the house were on. People had seen the lights and come to help me.

I got up slowly and walked to the door. There was only one man at the door. It was Keckwick. And behind him was his pony and trap. They were real and they were not harmed at all.

'I had to wait till the mist cleared,' said Keckwick. 'And when the mist cleared, the tide was in. I had to wait until the tide went out and the water left the cause-way.'

Then I looked at my watch and saw the time. It was two o'clock in the morning.

'It's very good of you to come here for me at this time,' I said.

'I would not have left you to stay here all night,' Keckwick said. 'No, no. I would not have left you here all night.'

'How did you get out of the mud . . . ?' I began to say. Then I knew. It had not been Keckwick. It had been someone else. But who? Who had been driving on the marshes on a dark November evening? Who?

Keckwick looked at me strangely.

'You'd better get in the trap,' he said. 'I'll drive you back.'

Keckwick knew that something strange had happened to me. But he was not going to ask me about it. And he did not want to hear about it. I got into the trap and we drove off.

I sat in the trap in a dream. A dream of horror and fear. I now knew the truth. But I did not want to believe it.

The woman in black was a ghost. And the child was a ghost too. I had seen the woman. I had heard the child. They had died long ago. But they did not rest in peace.

The innkeeper of the Gifford Arms had not gone to bed. He was waiting up for me. He let me in without a word. It was after three o'clock in the morning when I got to bed. I slept. But in my dreams, I heard the cry of a child. I stood once more in the white sea-mist. And always, near me, was the woman in black.

6

I Go Back

When I woke, the sun was shining. At first, I felt weak and ill. But after a bath and breakfast I felt better.

I was not going to run away. I had a job to do. I was afraid. I had seen and heard terrible things. But I was a young man. And young men forget easily.

I was going back to Eel Marsh House. I was going to look at Mrs Drablow's papers. But not today and not alone.

I wanted some exercise. I told the innkeeper I was going for a long walk.

'Can you ride a bicycle, sir?' he said. 'There's a bicycle here you can use.'

I was very pleased. Stella and I often rode bicycles into the country. Yes, an hour or two on a bicycle. That's what I needed! Then tomorrow, I would go back to Eel Marsh House. But not alone.

I decided to talk to Mr Jerome. He probably had a boy who worked in the office. The boy can help me, I thought. Together we will finish the job quickly.

I walked through the town to Mr Jerome's office. He did not look pleased to see me.

'The house is full of papers,' I said. 'I must look at them all. I need help.'

A look of fear came into Mr Jerome's face.

'I can't help you, Mr Kipps,' he said quickly.

'But can your office-boy help me?' I said.

'I don't have an office-boy,' Jerome answered.

'Well, any other boy in the town,' I said. 'I'll pay him of course.'

Mr Jerome stood up. His face was white.

'You will find no one to help you! No one!' he shouted.

'I think I understand you, Mr Jerome,' I said. 'No one in this town will stay at Eel Marsh House. Everyone is too afraid. Afraid of seeing . . .' I stopped.

'The woman in black?' Mr Jerome said.

'Yes,' I answered. 'I saw her again.'

'Where?' he whispered.

'In the graveyard behind Eel Marsh House. But she's not going to stop me – whoever she is – or was!'

I laughed. My laugh did not sound true.

'I must be brave, Mr Jerome,' I added. 'I'm not going to run away.'

'That's what I said . . .' the little man replied very quietly.

I did not understand him.

'Well, I'll go back alone,' I said. 'Perhaps I'll not see the woman again.'

'I pray that you do not,' Mr Jerome said slowly. 'I pray that you do not.'

I went back to the inn. I wrote a letter to Mr Bentley. I told him I wanted to stay for a few days. I said nothing about the woman in black.

Then I took the bicycle and rode off. The weather was perfect for cycling. The wind was cold. But the air was bright and clear.

I decided to ride west, away from the marshes. I was going to ride to the next village and have lunch there.

At the end of the town, I looked to the east. I was looking back to the water of the marshes. The marshes were pulling me back. I knew I had to go back to them. But not now. Not today.

Taking a deep breath, I turned my bicycle. My back was to the marshes now. I cycled away from the marshes along the country road.

7

Dinner With Mr Daily

I rode back to Crythin Gifford about four hours later. I was feeling happier. Eel Marsh House did not frighten me now. I knew I was brave enough to go there alone. The sea-mist and loneliness of the place had frightened me. How silly I had been to be afraid! That would not happen again.

I turned the corner into the town square. A big car was coming towards me. I stopped quickly. But I almost fell off the bicycle.

The car slowed down and stopped. Mr Samuel Daily looked out of the window.

'How are you, young man?' he called.

'Fine,' I said. 'I've had a good ride. I feel hungry and I'm looking forward to my dinner tonight!'

'And what about your business? Have you been out to the house?'

'Yes, of course,' I answered. 'It won't take me long.'

Mr Daily looked at me for a few moments. He said nothing.

'I'm enjoying the work,' I went on quickly. 'It's all very interesting. But there are many papers to look at.'

Mr Daily went on staring at me.

'Mr Kipps,' he said, 'those are brave words. But I don't believe them. Come to my house for dinner tonight. The innkeeper knows where I live.'

He sat back and the car drove on.

Mr Daily's words did not make me change my mind. I was going back to Eel Marsh House.

I went shopping in the town. I bought tea, coffee and bread. Then a large torch and rubber boots. I wanted to be ready for anything at Eel Marsh House.

I told the innkeeper what I was going to do.

'Tomorrow,' I said, 'I am going to go to Eel Marsh House. I am going to stay there for two nights. Can I use your bicycle?'

The innkeeper nodded. He said nothing. But he looked at me sadly.

In the evening, I cycled out to the Dailys' house. It was a very large house. Mr Daily was clearly a rich man.

Mr Daily and his wife gave me a friendly welcome. The food and drink were very good. All through dinner, Samuel Daily talked about himself. He had worked hard all his life. Now he owned land and houses.

I told him about Stella and our plans for the future.

After dinner, Mrs Daily left us. Until then, Mr Daily had not spoken about Mrs Drablow or Eel Marsh House.

He filled my glass and his own with wine.

'You're a fool to go on with it,' he said.

I knew what he meant.

'I've got a job to do, Mr Daily,' I said. 'And I want to do it well.'

'Listen to me, Arthur,' Daily said. 'There are stories about that place. Stories I'm not going to tell you. You'll hear them from other people. Perhaps you've heard them already. You've been out to the house, haven't you?'

'Yes, I've been there,' I answered. 'And I heard and saw things. Things I cannot understand.'

And then I told him everything.

Mr Daily listened carefully, but said nothing.

'I think the woman in black is a ghost,' I said. 'She made me afraid. She has the power to make people afraid. But that is all. She did me no harm.'

'And what about the pony and trap? The child's cry?' Daily asked.

Yes, I thought to myself, the child's cry was the worst of all. But I did not say that to Mr Daily.

'I'm not running away,' I said.

'You shouldn't go back,' Daily said.

'I must.'

'Then don't go alone.'

'No one will go with me,' I answered. 'I'll be all right. After all, Mrs Drablow lived there alone for sixty years!'

'Alone? I wonder,' Mr Daily said. He stood up. It was time for me to go. A servant brought my coat. When the man had left, Daily said, 'Are you really going back to that house?'

'I am,' I answered.

'Then if you must go, take a dog,' Daily said.

I laughed. 'I haven't got a dog!' I said.

'But I have a dog,' Daily answered. 'You can take her with you now.'

We walked out of the house together.

'Wait here a moment,' Daily said.

He walked round to the back of the house. I stood there smiling. I liked dogs. I was happy to have a dog with me in that empty old house.

28

After a few moments, Daily returned with a bright-eyed little dog.

'Take her,' he said. 'Bring her back when you've finished.'

'What's her name?'

'Spider.'

Hearing her name, the little dog wagged her tail.

'Thank you,' I said. 'Come on, girl. Come on, Spider!'

I began to walk away. The dog did not move. She looked at Daily.

'Go on, girl,' he said. Spider ran over to me at once.

Waving goodbye, I got on my bicycle. Then, with Spider running behind me, I rode back to the town.

I felt happy. Happy and safe. I was looking forward to the morning.

8

Sounds in the Night

Next day, the weather was good. At nine o'clock, Mr Bentley phoned from London.

'I've received your letter,' he said. 'You can stay for a few days. Send me any papers that look important. Leave the other papers in the house. Don't stay too long!'

'I'll finish the work as quickly as I can,' I answered. 'It's a strange old house,' I added.

'Mrs Drablow was a strange old woman,' Mr Bentley said. And he put the phone down.

By nine thirty, I was ready. There was a basket on the front of the bicycle. I put everything in the basket. I cycled off happily. The little dog, Spider, ran along behind me.

29

Hearing her name, the little dog wagged her tail.

The tide was coming in. Very soon it would cover the causeway. But that did not worry me. The air was clear. The sun was shining on the water. Sea-birds were flying and calling over the estuary.

I was soon at Eel Marsh House. I opened the windows. I lit fires in several rooms. Then I sat down at a big desk. The desk was in front of a window. I could see the sky, the marshes and the water.

I started work. The desk was full of papers. Most of them I threw away. But I kept a few to look at later.

I opened a cupboard and then another. Papers, more and more papers. I looked at everything carefully.

I worked hard all the morning. At two o'clock, I had some lunch. Then I called Spider and we went outside. I walked down to the old graveyard. Spider ran up and down. She was happy too.

I tried to read the words on the gravestones. But they were too old. Most of the words were difficult to read. The writing on one stone was a little clearer. Some letters were

worn away. But I could read most of the words.

Two people were buried here. I wondered who they had been.

I looked around me. It was a sad place. But I did not feel afraid.

The air was colder now. I went back to the house and Spider followed me. I was soon back at my desk again. I read paper after paper. But there was nothing important. I made myself a cup of tea. I went on working.

When it was dark, I closed the curtains. I turned on every light in the house. I put more coal on the fire.

I brought papers from other rooms. Papers, so many papers. Mrs Drablow had thrown nothing away in sixty years!

It was getting late, but I went on working. I'll be finished in a day and a half, I thought to myself. Then I'll return to London and my dear Stella.

At last, I was too tired to go on. I took a book to read in bed. Then, taking Spider with me, I went upstairs. I was going to sleep in a bedroom at the back of the house.

I read for about half an hour. Then I turned out the light. Spider was already asleep, near the bed.

Sometime later, I woke up. The moonlight was shining into the room. Why was I awake? What had happened? I sat up.

And then I saw Spider. The little dog was standing at the door. She was staring at the door, listening.

The little dog was terrified. And so was I. I listened too.

Yes, I could hear something. The sound came from somewhere inside the house. Bump. Bump. Bump. What was it?

Spider looked at me, growled and listened again. I got

slowly out of bed. My heart was beating fast. I opened the bedroom door. The passage outside was dark and empty.

Spider ran down the passage. I heard her sniffing at every closed door.

I heard the sound again. Bump. Bump. Bump. It came from a passage on the left. Very slowly, I began to walk towards the sound.

I opened the doors, one by one. Every room was dark and silent.

There was a door at the end of the passage. Spider sniffed under this door. Her growling became louder.

It was the door I had found locked on my first visit to the house. It was the only door I could not open. Yes, the sound came from behind this door. Bump. Bump. Bump.

I had heard this sound long ago. I had heard it when I was a child. What was it?

Spider howled. The frightened little dog pressed against my legs. We were both shaking with fear. And still the sound went on. Bump. Bump. Bump.

I heard another sound. It came from behind me. It came from the front of the house.

The bumping noise stopped. I turned away from the locked door. Slowly and carefully, I walked back to my bedroom.

Everything was quiet. The second sound had come from inside the house. I was sure of that. I looked round the room. Perhaps the sound had come from outside? I looked out of the window. I saw nothing, no one. The marshes were silver and grey in the moonlight. Did I hear a cry? I listened again. No.

I felt something warm against my leg. I bent down to stroke the little dog. She was quiet again.

The sound came from behind this door. Bump. Bump. Bump.

I listened. Everything was quiet. The house and the marshes were completely silent.

After a time, I went back to the closed door. I turned the handle. The door did not open. I pushed my shoulder against the door. It did not move. There was no keyhole in the door. I could not see into the room.

I went back to bed. But it was a long time before I fell asleep.

9

Behind the Door

The morning was cold and wet. The sky was covered with thick clouds. It was raining.

I was very tired. But after breakfast, I felt better. I went back to the locked door. I stood and listened. But I heard nothing.

At nine o'clock, I rode back along the causeway on the bicycle. Spider ran beside me.

There was a letter from Stella at the Gifford Arms inn. Her loving words made me feel very happy. In two or three more days we would be together again.

I walked round the town, buying more food. Then I rode back along the causeway. I was back at Eel Marsh House in time for lunch.

The clouds were thicker now. The sea-mist was coming in over the marshes.

Inside the house, it was already dark. I put on all the lights. But the house stayed dark and shadowy. My fears returned. I decided to go back to the town.

I went outside. There was some mist around the house. But I was able to see the causeway. However, it was completely covered by water. I could not return to Crythin Gifford that day.

So I whistled to Spider. She ran to me quickly. We both went back inside the house. I emptied papers from more cupboards. I started work again.

I worked hard for several hours. I found a packet of letters tied together. They looked interesting.

After supper, I sat down by the fire and opened the packet.

There were some papers and some letters. The letters were all in the same handwriting. They were signed 'Jennet' or 'J'. I remembered the gravestone I had seen. It was in the graveyard at the back of Eel Marsh House. One of the names on that gravestone had been Jennet! Was this the same Jennet?

There were dates on the letters. The letters had been written sixty years ago. Each letter began with the words, 'Dearest Alice'. Alice was Mrs Drablow's first name. All the letters were written to Mrs Alice Drablow.'

I looked through them quickly. Jennet was Mrs Drablow's younger sister.

I began to read the letters carefully. They were short and in simple language. They told a sad story.

Jennet was unmarried, but she was going to have a child. The child's father refused to marry Jennet and he left the country. Jennet did not know what to do. Her family refused to help her.

Then the child was born – a boy. For a few months, there were no letters. Then Jennet began writing again. And now her letters were full of anger.

The child is mine, Jennet wrote. *I will never give him to strangers.*

But Jennet was unmarried. She was poor and she could not keep the child. At last, she had to agree that Alice could take the boy.

In her last letter, Jennet wrote:

Love him, Alice. Love him as your own child. But remember, he is mine – mine! He can never be yours. Forgive me. My heart is breaking.

Poor Jennet, I thought. What a sad story! I began to look at the other papers. The first one was from a solicitor's office.

The paper was about a boy called Nathaniel. Nathaniel was the son of Jennet Humfrye. Nathaniel had been adopted by Thomas and Alice Drablow of Eel Marsh House.

Alice Drablow was Jennet Humfrye's married sister. Nathaniel had been given the name Drablow.

So the child, Nathaniel Drablow, had lived here, I thought. Away from the mother who loved him.

I thought for a few moments about Jennet Humfrye and her sad life. Then I picked up the next paper.

At that moment, Spider growled. The little dog was standing at the door. Every hair on her body was stiff with fear.

I sat there for a few moments, frozen with fright. Then I stood up. If this was a ghost, I must face it.

I made myself walk to the door. I opened it. Spider rushed out of the room and up the stairs. I heard her run along the passage. She stopped. I knew she had stopped outside the locked door!

I heard the sound again. Bump. Bump. Bump.

I knew what I must do. I must open that door. There was

37

an axe in the wood-shed. I must get that axe.

Taking my torch, I stepped outside the house. It was very dark. But I found the wood-shed. And the axe.

As I was walking back, I heard the sound of the pony and trap. It came from the front of the house. Had Keckwick come back for me?

No one was there, no one at all. I could still hear the pony and trap. But now the sound was coming from the marshes.

I stood there, Spider beside me. I was terribly afraid. Again, I heard the sounds of the water and the mud. I heard the pony shriek. I heard the child's awful cry. And then, silence.

I was shaking now. My mouth was dry with fear. I had heard these sounds before. The pony and child were not alive. I knew this. A pony and trap and all the people in it had sunk beneath the water.

Spider began to howl and howl. I put down the axe and the torch and picked up the little dog. I carried her into the house. She was afraid and so was I.

After a few moments, the dog jumped out of my arms. She ran upstairs, towards the locked door. I hurried outside, picked up the axe and torch and followed her.

The sound was louder now. When I reached the door, I saw why. The door of the locked room was open – wide open. I thought I was going to die of fear.

The dog ran inside the room. The bumping sound went on. And now I remembered. I knew what the sound was.

When I was a child, my mother had a rocking-chair. Sometimes I couldn't sleep. Then my mother held me in her arms. She sat in the chair and rocked me back and forwards. Bump. Bump. Bump. That was the sound made by the rocking-chair on the floor.

I was no longer afraid. The sound meant peace and rest.

There was evil in that room. I knew that. But it had gone away. Perhaps it was my happy thoughts. They had driven the evil away from that place. Holding the torch in front of me, I walked into the room.

I pressed the light switch. Nothing happened. But my torch was powerful. I shone the bright torch round the room.

The room had been a child's bedroom. There was a small bed in one corner. A tall rocking-chair stood in front of the fireplace. The chair was rocking gently.

But there was no one there. The room was empty. No one had passed me in the passage. There was no other door. I shone my torch at the window. It was shut. There were two wooden bars across it. The chair stopped moving. There was complete silence.

The little room was clean and tidy. There were sheets and pillows on the bed. I opened a chest and a cupboard. They were both full of clothes. Clothes for a boy of six or seven. The clothes were beautifully made. But they were old-fashioned clothes – clothes of sixty years ago.

The room was full of children's toys. They were neat and tidy. There was no dust on them at all.

I saw toy soldiers and a sailing-ship. There were games, paints and books. All things that little boys love.

They had been here for sixty years. But everything was neat, tidy and clean.

There was nothing frightening in this room. Only a feeling of sadness – a feeling of something lost. I felt sad, very sad.

A tall rocking-chair stood in front of the fireplace.
The chair was rocking gently.

I went slowly out of the room. Spider followed and I closed the door. I felt too tired to do any more work.

I had a hot drink and went upstairs. The door to the child's bedroom was still closed. Everything was quiet. I went into my bedroom and closed the door.

10

Terror on the Marshes

That night, there was a very strong wind. It whistled and howled around the house. The windows shook. I slept, woke and slept again.

Then suddenly I was wide awake. I thought I heard a cry. The wind blew more loudly. Then I heard the cry again. It was the cry of a child. A cry for help. The cry of a child dying in the marshes. For how many years had the child cried out?

Rest in peace, I prayed. But that child could not.

I could not sleep. I got up. I opened the bedroom door. Spider followed me into the passage.

Suddenly two things happened. Someone or something went past me. The wind howled, louder than ever. And all the lights went out.

I stood there in the darkness. I could not move. Who had gone by? Who was in the house with me? I had seen and heard nothing. But I was sure of one thing. Someone had gone along the passage to the child's bedroom. Someone dead for many years – a ghost.

I had to have a light. I walked back carefully into my bedroom.

I went slowly to the table near my bed. I found the torch and picked it up. But it slipped from my fingers. It fell and broke on the floor.

Spider came close and touched my hand. As I held the little dog, the wind howled again. And once more, louder than the wind, I heard the child's cry.

I could not sleep. I must have a light, I thought. I cannot stay here in the dark. Then I remembered. I had seen a candle in the child's bedroom.

For a long time, I did not move. There was something evil in the child's bedroom. But I had to go back to get that candle.

I went down the passage slowly. I opened the door of the child's bedroom. Everything was quiet. I found the candle and picked it up.

Now I was in the bedroom, I was not afraid. But I felt sad. I had a feeling of something lost. Someone who had died. I had never had that feeling before. Why did I have it now?

After a few minutes, I walked slowly out of the room. I closed the door. At once, the sadness left me.

In my bedroom, I found some matches. I lit the candle. I opened my book and began to read. Some time later, I fell asleep. When I woke up again, the sky was light. It was morning.

Spider was standing at the door. She wagged her tail and looked at me. The dog wanted to go out.

I got up and dressed quickly. Spider ran to the front door.

I opened the door. Spider ran out happily. The air was very cold. Then I heard a whistle. A high, clear sound.

Spider heard it too. Before I could stop her, she was running. She was running away from the house onto the marshes. I called and called, but she did not hear me. I watched the little dog running on and on. But who had whistled? The marshes were completely empty.

Then I saw the dog slow down and stop. I knew at once what had happened. The poor animal was caught in the mud. The mud was pulling the dog down. Pulling her down deeper and deeper.

I could not let the little dog die. Without thinking, I ran out across the marshes towards her.

The cold wind blew in my face. I could not see clearly. My feet stuck in the mud. I pulled myself free. The tide was coming in quickly.

I called out to the dog. Most of her body was now under mud and water. I could not get any nearer to her.

I could do nothing. We will both die here, in this terrible place, I thought. No, it could not happen!

Very carefully, I lay down. I stretched forward, little by little. The dog sank deeper into the mud.

Just in time, I got hold of the leather collar round the dog's neck. I pulled and pulled.

At last, the dog was free from the mud! We lay there side by side, wet and muddy. We were safe, thank God. The dog was alive and so was I.

How long we lay there, I do not know. At last, I got up. I began to walk slowly back to the house.

As I got nearer to the house, I looked up. I saw the window of the child's bedroom. Someone was standing there, looking out. It was the woman in black.

She stared at me. The hate in her eyes was terrible.

43

I got hold of the leather collar round the dog's neck.
I pulled and pulled.

I began to shake. Somehow, I reached the front door of the house.

Then, to my horror, I heard the sound I feared most – the sound of a pony and trap.

11

I Leave Eel Marsh House

The next thing I knew, I was lying on a couch in the sitting-room. Mr Daily was leaning over me. I tried to sit up, but I couldn't. I did not know what had happened to me.

'The trap – the pony and trap,' I said.

'Oh, that was me,' Samuel Daily said with a smile. 'I've come here in a pony and trap. It's safer than a car on that causeway. What's the matter? What did you think?'

'I've . . . I've heard another . . .' I said.

'Keckwick, perhaps.'

'No, not Keckwick,' I said. 'But why did you come?'

'I was worried about you,' said Daily. 'It's a good thing I came. People have drowned in those marshes, you know.'

'Yes. I was nearly pulled under. And the dog . . .'

Then I remembered.

'Spider!' I cried. 'Where's Spider? Did she . . .?'

'She's safe,' Daily said. 'She's here.'

At the sound of her name, the little dog jumped up and wagged her tail.

'Now I'm taking you home with me,' said Daily. 'You can't stay here.'

For a few moments, I said nothing. I remembered what had happened to me. I knew that the woman in black was a ghost. But why was she here? I knew there was evil here. And sadness too. Why? I wanted to know. And I had to finish my work too.

'Thank you, Mr Daily,' I said after a few moments. 'I want to leave Eel Marsh House. But what about my work? I must look at all Mrs Drablow's papers. I don't think there's anything important. But they must be looked at.'

'I found some letters last night,' I went on. 'They looked interesting. I'll bring them with me.'

Very slowly, I got up. I picked up the packet of letters from the desk. Then I went upstairs to get my things. My fear had gone. I was leaving Eel Marsh House. If I came back, I would not come alone.

I packed my bag and left the room. I decided to have one last look at the child's bedroom.

The door was open. But I was sure I had closed it.

I could hear Mr Daily downstairs. I was safe. I walked slowly towards the open door.

Then I stopped. Did I want to go in? She had been here. I had seen her.

I pushed open the door.

I could not believe my eyes. Everything in the room was broken and torn. The cupboards were all open. Toys, clothes and books lay on the floor. They had been thrown there by some terrible power. Everything was destroyed.

Everything except the rocking-chair. It had been pushed into the centre of the room. The chair was not moving now. Who or what had done this terrible thing?

Everything in the room was broken and torn.

Feeling ill and shaking, I got into the trap beside Mr Daily. He knew that something had happened. But he did not ask any questions.

He put Spider on my knees. I held the dog tightly. Then we drove off away from the house, across the Nine Lives Causeway.

Everything was grey and quiet. There was no colour, no sound. I looked back at Eel Marsh House. No one was watching us. The house stood there, grey and terrible.

As we crossed the estuary, I turned my eyes away. I did not want to see that terrible place again.

12

The Death Certificates

The Dailys invited me to stay with them for a few days. I agreed thankfully. After a few days, I would go straight back to London. Not to Eel Marsh House. I would never go back there again.

But I was angry. I had not finished my work. The woman in black had stopped me.

Then I remembered the papers I had brought with me from Eel Marsh House. The letters told a sad story. I wanted to know how the story ended.

I read the letters again. Poor Jennet! She had loved her child so much. But she was unmarried. She could not keep her boy. She had to give him to her sister, Mrs Drablow. The child had lived at Eel Marsh House. What had happened to him?

I picked up the other papers and looked at them. They were death certificates.

The first was for a boy. *Name: Nathaniel Drablow. Age: six years. Cause of death: drowning.*

I looked at the second certificate. *Rosa Judd – nursemaid. Cause of death: drowning.*

On both certificates, the date of death was the same.

I held the death certificates tightly in my hand. I felt myself grow cold. I got up and walked about the room.

Then I looked at the last piece of paper. It was another death certificate. This time, the date was twelve years later.

The certificate was for *Jennet Humfrye, unmarried. Age: thirty-six years. Cause of death: heart failure.*

I sat down in my chair. One thing was clear – the woman in black was Jennet Humfrye or her ghost. I did not believe in ghosts, but I had seen her.

And now I knew something else. Long, long ago, a pony and trap had left the causeway. It had sunk down in the mud of the marshes. A child and a nursemaid had been drowned.

Jennet, the boy's mother, had died twelve years after her son. I knew where they were buried. They were buried in the old graveyard behind Eel Marsh House.

Nathaniel had slept in that bedroom. For sixty years the bedroom had stayed the same. Those clothes, those toys, were his.

Jennet Humfrye was the woman in black. Her hatred had never left her. Her ghost followed anyone who went near Eel Marsh House.

What power did Jennet Humfrye have? Could the dead harm the living? I did not know the answer. I wanted to find out the answer.

13

'Nothing Can Happen Now . . .'

That evening, after dinner, I had a long talk with Mr Daily. Spider was asleep in front of the bright fire.

Daily gave me a drink and I began my story. I told him everything I had seen and heard.

When I had finished, there was silence. My story was told. I was at peace.

'Well, young man,' Samuel Daily said at last, 'you've had an unhappy time here.'

'Yes,' I said. 'But it's finished. Those things can't harm me now, can they?'

Daily said nothing. But he looked unhappy.

'Nothing can happen now,' I said with a smile. 'I'm never going back there. All is well.'

Daily said nothing. I began to feel worried.

'Can there be anything else?' I asked. 'Nothing will harm me now, will it?'

'Not you, perhaps,' Daily said slowly. 'You can leave. But the rest of us must stay here. We have to live with it.'

'With what? Live with what?' I asked.

'This town has lived in fear for a long time,' Daily said. 'For more than fifty years. Terrible things have happened. But people don't talk about them.'

My heart beat faster. I did not want to know any more. But Mr Daily went on talking.

'You know most of the story. But not all of it,' he said.

'Jennet Humfrye sent her boy to Eel Marsh House. To her sister, Mrs Drablow. At first, Jennet went away to another part of the country. But she had to be near her son. She came back to Crythin.'

'She got work in the town. But Alice Drablow refused to see her. She refused to let Jennet see the child. Jennet's anger was terrible. So Alice Drablow allowed her to visit the house. But she must never tell the boy who she was.'

'But the boy looked like his mother. And he loved her. He loved his mother more than Alice Drablow. Jennet wanted her son back. She planned to take him away from Eel Marsh House.'

'Then the accident happened. The sea-mist came down suddenly. The boy and the nursemaid were drowned. The driver of the trap too – he was Keckwick's father. And the boy's little dog. They were all drowned,' Daily said.

'All drowned,' I said slowly.

'Yes. And Jennet saw everything. She saw everything from the bedroom window.'

'Oh, my God!' I said quietly.

'Jennet Humfrye began to go mad,' Samuel Daily said. 'She was mad with sorrow and anger. She said her sister had killed her son.'

'Then poor Jennet became ill. She became thin and pale. Children were frightened of her. When she died, people began to see her ghost.'

'There is something more terrible. Each time she is seen, something else happens.'

'What?' I asked.

'A child has died. Either by illness, or in a terrible accident.'

'Any child? A child in the town?'

'Any child,' said Daily. 'Once, it was Jerome's child. You

51

may find this hard to believe, Arthur,' Daily added. 'But it is true.'

I looked into his eyes.

'I believe it, Mr Daily,' I said. 'I believe it.'

That night, I slept badly. I woke up again and again. I had terrible dreams. When morning came, I felt weak and ill.

I was very ill for five days. In my illness, I had terrible dreams. In my dreams, the woman in black pushed her terrible face near mine. She sat on my bed, watching, watching.

I heard the cry of her dying child, again and again. I heard the bump, bump, of the rocking-chair.

Slowly, I got better. At the end of twelve days, I was well again.

It was a day of winter sunshine. I was sitting downstairs by the open window. Spider lay at my feet. A bird was singing in the garden. I listened to it with peace in my heart.

I heard the sound of a car and voices. I heard footsteps. The door behind me opened.

'Arthur?' a voice said quietly. It was a voice I knew. I turned quickly. My dear Stella was walking towards me. She had come to take me home!

The next morning, Stella and I left together. We did not go back into the town. We went straight to the railway station in Mr Daily's car.

The Dailys had looked after me well. I was sad to say goodbye to them. They agreed to visit us in London. And I was sad to say goodbye to Spider.

There was a question I had to ask Mr Daily. I waited until

In my dreams, the woman in black pushed her terrible face near mine.

Stella was saying goodbye to Mrs Daily.

'There is something I must know,' I said to Mr Daily. 'You told me that a child always died . . .'

'Yes, always.'

'Then has a child . . .?'

'No, nothing has happened,' Daily said. 'A child hasn't died – yet.'

'Then pray God, the woman in black has gone for ever,' I said. 'Pray God her power is at an end.'

'Yes, yes,' Daily said. 'We all hope that.'

I began to feel sorry for poor Jennet Humfrye. She had lost her son. Her sorrow and anger had made her mad. Now Mrs Drablow was dead. Eel Marsh House was empty. Wasn't that the end? Could Jennet Humfrye rest in peace now?

The train was waiting. I said goodbye to the Dailys.

Thank God, my business in Crythin Gifford was finished.

14

The Story Ends

That is nearly the end of my story. I have one last thing to write. But it is the most terrible thing of all.

For days and nights, I have sat at my desk here at Monk's Piece. I have tried to write down the rest of my story. But my tears have stopped me. My dear wife, Esmé, sees I am unhappy. But she doesn't know why.

But now I am ready to finish my story.

Stella and I returned to London. Six weeks later, we were married. My wife and I were not rich. But we were happy.

A year later, our son was born. Our happiness was complete. I did not think of the past. And I had no more bad dreams.

Another year passed. Our son was about a year old. It was a sunny Sunday afternoon. Stella and I took our boy to one of the parks in London.

Everyone was happy. The sun was shining. Children were running about on the green grass. Music was playing. Everyone was enjoying the holiday.

Someone was giving rides to children in a pony and trap. Our son saw the trap. He shouted and pointed at it.

It was a small trap. There was room for only two passengers. So Stella took the boy. I stood watching them happily.

The trap went behind some trees. I looked around me at the happy people.

And then I saw her. The woman in black. She was standing near a big tree.

She looked at me. There was no mistake. I was looking at the white face and staring eyes of Jennet Humfrye.

My body was icy cold. I could not move. I saw the terrible hate in the woman's eyes.

At that moment, the pony and trap came back. It came towards me, between the tall trees. My dear Stella was smiling. Our little son was laughing. I stepped forward.

They passed the tree where the woman in black was standing.

She moved quickly in front of the pony. The frightened pony shrieked. It turned and ran back under the trees. The driver could not stop it.

I was looking at the white face and staring eyes of
Jennet Humfrye.

There was a terrible crash. Then silence. The woman in black had gone. But my darling Stella and my dear son lay on the grass. They did not move.

Our baby son was dead. Stella's body was broken. But she did not die. Not then. For ten long months, I sat by her bed. Then Stella died at last from her terrible injuries.

They asked me for my story. I have told it. There is nothing more to write.

Points for Understanding

1

1 Where does Arthur Kipps live? Who does he live with?
2 Why do the children's stories not frighten Arthur?
3 Why is Arthur not able to tell a story?
4 What does Arthur decide to do?

2

1 How old was Arthur when his story began? What was his work?
2 Mr Bentley asked Arthur to go to Mrs Drablow's funeral.
    (a) What was the name of Mrs Drablow's house?
    (b) Where was it?
    (c) What was Arthur to do after the funeral?
3 'What a strange address!' I said. What was Mr Bentley's reply?
4 Why did Arthur write a note to Stella?
5 'Didn't Mrs Drablow have any friends?' I asked.
    (a) Why did Arthur ask Mr Daily this question?
    (b) What was Mr Daily's reply?
6 'Are you trying to frighten me, Mr Daily?' Arthur asked.
    (a) What was Mr Daily's reply?
    (b) How did Mr Daily show he was a kind man?
7 Did Arthur sleep well at the Gifford Arms? Why was he thankful for that one night's good sleep?

3

1 Describe the countryside round the town of Crythin Gifford.
2 Who was Mr Jerome?
3 Describe the woman Arthur saw standing at the back of the church.
4 What happened when Arthur tried to point the woman out to Mr Jerome?
5 Who was going to take Arthur to Eel Marsh House?
6 Why was it not always possible to go to Eel Marsh House?

4

1 Describe the journey across Nine Lives Causeway.
2 Describe Eel Marsh House.
3 How long could Arthur stay before the tide covered the causeway again?
4 Arthur saw a woman in the churchyard. Why did he shake with fear?
5 What kind of furniture did Arthur find in every room?
6 Why would Arthur have a lot of work to do in the house?

5

1 The sea-mist was moving quickly over the marshes.
   (a) Why was Arthur afraid to go on walking?
   (b) Why did he think Keckwick was coming towards him?
   (c) What terrible sound did he hear next?
2 What time did Keckwick come for Arthur?
3 I now knew the truth, Arthur thought to himself. What was the truth?

6

1 Why could Arthur not get anyone to help him with his work?
2 Where did Arthur go after he saw Mr Jerome?

7

1 Who did Arthur meet when he returned to Crythin Gifford?
2 What advice was Arthur given? Why wouldn't Arthur accept the advice?
3 Who was Spider?

8

1   Arthur was able to read some of the writing on one gravestone.
    (a) How many people had been buried in the grave?
    (b) How were they related?
2   Why did Arthur get out of bed in the middle of the night?
3   There was a locked room Arthur could not get into. Why did he want to get into this room?

9

1   Arthur began to read the letters carefully.
    (a) What was the name of the person who had signed the letters?
    (b) Who were the letters written to?
2   The letters told a sad story. What was the story?
3   Then the letters became full of anger. Why was the writer angry?
4   The paper was about a boy called Nathaniel.
    (a) Who was Nathaniel's mother?
    (b) Who had adopted him?
5   What sound did Arthur suddenly hear coming again from the locked room?
6   Why did Arthur go outside to the wood-shed?
7   What did Arthur know had happened sometime in the past?
8   The bumping sound was louder now.
    (a) Why was the bumping sound louder?
    (b) What was making the sound?
    (c) What other things did Arthur see in the child's bedroom?

10

1 Why did Arthur pray: 'Rest in peace'?
2 Suddenly two things happened. What two things?
3 Why did Arthur have to go back to the child's bedroom? Why did he not want to go back there?
4 Why did Spider run out onto the marshes?
5 How did Arthur save Spider?
6 'As I got nearer the house, I looked up.'
    (a) Who did Arthur see?
    (b) Why did he begin to shake?
    (c) What did he hear?

11

1 Who was in the house when Arthur woke up?
2 Why had Arthur decided to leave Eel Marsh House?
3 Arthur went to have one last look in the child's bedroom. What had changed?
4 Why did Arthur turn his eyes away as he left the estuary?

12

1 Where did Arthur stay for a few days?
2 What information was on the death certificates?
3 What was the question Arthur did not know the answer to?

13

1 'Then the accident happened,' said Mr Daily.
    (a) What happened in the accident?
    (b) Where did Jennet see the accident from?
2 What happened after Jennet died?
3 What else happens each time Jennet's ghost is seen?
4 Who had come to take Arthur home?
5 'Then has a child . . .?'
    (a) Complete Arthur's question.
    (b) What was Mr Daily's reply?

14

1   What stopped Arthur writing the rest of his story?
2   How was Arthur's happiness made complete?
3   Where did Arthur and Stella go one sunny Sunday afternoon?
4   Someone was giving rides to children . . .
   (a) What were they giving rides in?
   (b) Who did Arthur see standing near a big tree?
   (c) What happened next?

Exercises

Background

Arthur Kipps worked for a law firm in London. He was a solicitor. The story begins in about 1930.

An old lady had died. Her name was Alice Drablow. She had lived at Eel Marsh House on the coast of Yorkshire. Eel Marsh House was close to a village called Crythin Gifford.

Arthur Kipps went to her house. He looked at her papers.

The house was strange and lonely, but in a beautiful place. It was at the end of a causeway across a marsh. Twice a day the sea covered the causeway. During these times it was not possible to get from the village to the house – or from the house to the village.

Arthur saw a strange woman. She was dressed all in black. Her face was very pale.

He asked people: 'Who is the woman in black?' They did not answer. They were afraid.

Tick the best answer.

1   What is a law firm?
a   ☐ It is a company that makes guns.
b   ☑ It is a company that handles legal matters.
c   ☐ It is a local police office.

2   Where did Arthur work?
a   ☐ In London, but he often had to travel to Yorkshire.
b   ☐ In Yorkshire.
c   ☐ In London, but he had had to go to Yorkshire on business.

3   What is a solicitor?
a   ☐ A person who handles legal papers.
b   ☐ A person who counts money.
c   ☐ A person who buys and sells houses.

4   When does this story begin?
a   ☐ In the late nineteenth century.
b   ☐ In the first half of the twentieth century.
c   ☐ In the present day.

5 Where does this story mainly take place?
a ☐ In an area called Yorkshire in England.
b ☐ In London.
c ☐ At a house called Monk's Piece.

6 Eel Marsh House was on the coast of Yorkshire. What does this tell us?
a ☐ It was in the north of Yorkshire.
b ☐ It was inland.
c ☐ It was next to the sea.

7 What is a causeway?
a ☐ It is a raised road across wet land.
b ☐ It is a bridge you pay to cross.
c ☐ It is a narrow road across dry land.

8 Twice a day it was not possible to cross the causeway. Why?
a ☐ Because it closed in the evening and at lunchtime.
b ☐ Because when the tide was in, the sea covered it.
c ☐ Because of special local laws.

9 Which word tells us that Eel Marsh House was unusual?
a ☐ beautiful
b ☐ lonely
c ☐ strange

10 What is a marsh?
a ☐ An area of land covered with trees.
b ☐ An area of wet land.
c ☐ An area of land suitable for building houses.

11 Why did Arthur go to Eel Marsh House?
a ☐ To write a will for Alice Drablow.
b ☐ To visit Alice Drablow.
c ☐ To sort out Alice Drablow's legal affairs.

12 Why didn't people answer Arthur's question: 'Who is the woman in black?'
a ☐ Because Arthur came from London.
b ☐ Because Arthur was a solicitor.
c ☐ Because they were frightened of something.

Words From the Story

Write each word from the box next to the correct meaning.

estuary   will   funeral   gravestone   property   pony   grave   tide
bonnet   rocking-chair   death certificate   torch

1 *property* ....   something you have and own, especially a house or apartment

2 ....   a legal paper; it says who will have your money and property when you die

3 ....   a ceremony when a dead person is buried or burned

4 ....   a hole in the ground where a dead person's body is put

5 ....   a stone marker put on a grave; it shows the dead person's name, date of birth and death

6 ....   the mouth of a river – where it flows into the sea

7 ....   the movement of the sea towards the land and away from the land

8 ....   a small horse – often used to pull an open carriage called a trap

9 ....   a small electric light

10 ....   a kind of chair that moves backwards and forwards

11 ....   an old-fashioned woman's hat

12 ....   an official paper; it says when and how someone died

The Funeral

Complete the gaps. Use each word in the box once.

> saw   gone   were   thought   have   heard   standing   went
> looked   dressed   see   talking   turned   covered   stopped
> raised   left   was   closed   opened   followed   asked   walked

As we ¹.......walked....... through the square, people stared at us.
They stopped ².................................... . No one smiled.

The church stood in an old graveyard. There ³....................................
old gravestones on either side of a long path.

It ⁴.................................... very cold inside the church. Mr Jerome and I
were the only people at the funeral. Poor Mrs Drablow, I
⁵.................................... . Didn't she ⁶.................................... any friends
at all? Then I ⁷.................................... a sound behind me. I
⁸.................................... . A young woman was ⁹.................................... at
the back of the church. She was ¹⁰.................................... in old-
fashioned black clothes – clothes of sixty years ago. A large, old-
fashioned bonnet ¹¹.................................... her face. She
¹².................................... her head and ¹³.................................... at me.
The young woman's face was white and very thin. How ill she looked!

When we ¹⁴.................................... the church I looked for the woman.
But I did not ¹⁵.................................... her. Then in the graveyard, I
¹⁶.................................... her again. In the sunshine her face was whiter
and thinner.

I ¹⁷.................................... my eyes to pray. When I
¹⁸.................................... them, the woman had ¹⁹.................................... .
Beyond the graveyard I saw the estuary. And beyond the estuary was
the open sea.

The funeral was over. I ²⁰.................................. Mr Jerome from the churchyard.

'Who was that young woman?' I ²¹.................................. him. Mr Jerome ²².................................. and looked at me.

'Young woman?' he said.

'Yes, a young woman. She was dressed in black and she looked very ill.'

Mr Jerome's face ²³.................................. white.

'I did not see a young woman,' he said.

People in the Story

Write the correct name next to each description below.

| Alice Drablow | Mr Daily | Arthur Kipps | Stella |
| Esmé | Jennet Humfrye |

1 .... He was a young solicitor from London at the time of the story.

2 .... She married Arthur but was killed with her son in a pony and trap.

3 .... She was Arthur's second wife.

4 .... She lived in a strange old house in Yorkshire. She and her husband adopted her sister's son.

5 .... Her son drowned, and she died twelve years later.

6 .... He was a wealthy Yorkshire man and he had a dog called Spider.

Making Sentences 1

Match the beginnings on the left with the endings on the right to make full sentences.

1 I could not open the door   I heard a child's cry.

2 I pulled up the blinds   along the causeway.

3 I decided to walk back   but it was a long time before I fell asleep.

4 The sea-mist and the loneliness of the place   because it was locked.

5 I went back to bed   called Nathaniel.

6 The paper was about a boy   at every window.

7 And once more, louder than the wind,   the woman in black was Jennet Humfrye.

8 At the sound of her name   had frightened me.

9 One thing was clear –   something else happens.

10 Each time she is seen,   the little dog jumped up and wagged her tail.

Making Sentences 2

Write questions for the answers.

1 *How many people were there at Alice Drablow's funeral?*
....
There were only two people at Alice Drablow's funeral – Mr Jerome and Arthur Kipps.

2 *Who*
....
Keckwick drove Arthur to Eel Marsh House.

3 *How long*
....
Arthur stayed there for several hours.

4 *What*
....
He heard the sound of a pony and trap.

5 *Where*
....
The sound came from the marsh.

6 *Why*
....
Keckwick was late collecting Arthur because of the mist and the tide.

7 *Who*
....
The woman in black was a ghost.

8 *Who*
....
Mr Daily gave Arthur a dog.

9 *What*
....
The dog's name was Spider.

10 *Why*
....
Mr Daily gave it to him because he did not want Arthur to be alone in Eel Marsh House.

Multiple Choice

Tick the best answer.

1 Alice Drablow was …
a ☐ the woman in black.
b ☑ the person who owned Eel Marsh House.
c ☐ the wife of the Gifford Arms innkeeper.
d ☐ the wife of Arthur Kipps.

2 Jennet Humfrye was …
a ☐ the woman who lived in Eel Marsh House.
b ☐ the nursemaid who drowned in the marsh.
c ☐ the sister of Alice Drablow.
d ☐ the maid at the Gifford Arms.

3 Nathaniel Drablow was …
a ☐ the son of Alice Drablow.
b ☐ the son of Stella.
c ☐ the son of the nursemaid.
d ☐ the son of Jennet Humfrye.

4 Whose was the locked room at Eel Marsh House?
a ☐ Alice Drablow's.
b ☐ Nathaniel Drablow's.
c ☐ The nursemaid's.
d ☐ Jennet Humfrye's.

5 Why did Nathaniel have the surname Drablow?
a ☐ Because his mother's name was Drablow.
b ☐ Because his father's name was Drablow.
c ☐ Because his mother changed his name.
d ☐ Because his aunt and uncle adopted him.

6 Who was drowned in the marsh?
a ☐ Keckwick, the driver of the pony and trap.
b ☐ Thomas and Alice Drablow.
c ☐ Nathaniel Drablow and his nursemaid.
d ☐ Jennet Humfrye and her son.

7 Who did Jennet Humfrye blame for the death of her son?
a ☐ Her sister.
b ☐ The nursemaid.
c ☐ Her mother.
d ☐ The driver of the trap.

8 Where were Jennet and Nathaniel buried?
a ☐ In the churchyard in Crythin Gifford.
b ☐ In the marsh.
c ☐ Inside the church of Crythin Gifford.
d ☐ Behind Eel Marsh House.

9 Who or what was the woman in black?
a ☐ The ghost of Alice Drablow.
b ☐ The ghost of Jennet Humfrye.
c ☐ The ghost of the nursemaid.
d ☐ The ghost of Jennet Humfrye's mother.

10 Where did Arthur first see the woman in black?
a ☐ In the locked room at Eel Marsh House.
b ☐ In the graveyard behind Eel Marsh House.
c ☐ In the graveyard at Crythin Gifford.
d ☐ In the church at Crythin Gifford.

11 Why were the villagers afraid of the woman in black?
a ☐ Because whenever they saw her something bad happened.
b ☐ Because she came into people's houses and moved their furniture.
c ☐ Because her face was so ugly and terrifying.
d ☐ Because they often heard her screams at night.

12 What did Arthur ask Mr Daily before he left Crythin Gifford?
a ☐ He asked whether anyone had seen the woman in black again.
b ☐ He asked whether Eel Marsh House was still empty.
c ☐ He asked whether a child had died.
d ☐ He asked whether Mr Daily had ever seen the woman in black.

13 Who lost a child after someone saw the woman in black?
a ☐ Mr Jerome and Arthur Kipps.
b ☐ Mr Bentley and Keckwick.
c ☐ Mr Daily and Thomas Drablow.
d ☐ Arthur Kipps and Keckwick.

Published by Macmillan Heinemann ELT
Between Towns Road, Oxford OX4 3PP
Macmillan Heinemann ELT is an imprint of
Macmillan Publishers Limited
Companies and representatives throughout the world
Heinemann is a registered trademark of Pearson Education, used under licence.

ISBN 978 0 2300 3745 8
ISBN 978 1 4050 7701 9 (with CD pack)

The Woman in Black © Susan Hill 1983
First published Hamish Hamilton Guided Readers

This retold version by Margaret Tarner for Macmillan Readers
First published 1990
Text © Margaret Tarner 1990, 1992, 2001, 2005
Design and illustration © Macmillan Publishers Limited 2005

This edition first published 2005

Illustrated by Annabel Large
Typography by Adrian Hodgkins
Original cover template design by Jackie Hill
Cover illustration by Graham Humphreys

Printed in Thailand
2011 2010 2009
6   5   4   3   2

with CD pack
2011 2010 2009
10 9   8   7   6